# THE FOOL.

by
Jennifer Jean

*The Fool* © 2013 by Jennifer Jean. All rights reserved.
Big Table Publishing Company retains right to reprint. Permission to reprint must be obtained by the author who owns copyright. Some of the poems in this book have appeared previously:

*Awakenings Review* – "In the War"
*Denver Quarterly* – "Last but First"
*Endicott Review* – "Brief History of Breath"
*Like One: Poems for Boston* – "Some thoughts on rocks."
*Linebreak's* <u>Two Weeks: an Audio Anthology</u> – "The Women"
*The Living Poetry Project 2012* – "Vespers"
*MassPoetry* – reprint "Passing Time" and "The Prisoner" and "Rooting"
*Megaera* – "Structural Integrity"
*The Mom Egg Review: VOX MOM* – "Trust"
*North Dakota Quarterly* – "Wreck Things"
*Plath Profiles: volume 5* – "Her Children"
*Poets/Artists* – "Getting to Know You"
*The Poetry Dress: an art instillation* – "Rooting"
*Relief: a Quarterly of Christian Expression* – "Grace" and "Zero Point"
*Southern California Review* – "Garden Apartments in Canoga Park, Calif."
*SSU Winfisky Gallery exhibit: Standing On It* – "Some thoughts on rocks:"
*Tidal Basin Review* – "Passing Time" and "The Prisoner"
*UC Magazine* – reprint "The Prisoner"
*The Wilderness House Review* – "Little's Lane in Peabody, Mass."
*Zymbol* – "There was this egg."

Photo credit: Masao Okano
Cover Design: Youngshim Gontijo
Cover Layout: Christopher Reilley

ISBN: 978-0-9830666-0-6

Also by Jennifer Jean:
*The Archivist*
*In the War*
*Fishwife*

Printed in the United States of America
by Big Table Publishing Company  Boston, MA

bigtablepublishing.com

Acknowledgements:

The Fool encounters many folks on her journey to becoming a fully realized being. In much the same way, there has been a multitude helping me nurture this book. Copious thank yous: to my publisher Robin "kick-ass fire-starter" Stratton, to my *anam cara* Laurette Folk, to my po-biz guru and dear friend January O'Neil, and to the funky-bunch at the Salem Writers Group (a partial list: J.D. Scrimgeour, Kevin Carey, Colleen Michaels, Jen Martelli, Margaret Young, Cindy Veach-Lappetito, Dawn Paul, Danielle Jones-Pruett—with special thanks to Melissa Varnavas for help with "Passing Time"); as well, big thank yous to this trio of poetic awesomeness: Aimee Nezhukumatathil, Afaa Michael Weaver, and Fred Marchant; also, to Michelle Gallant who keeps me in my breath, to the folks at the Morning Garden Writers Retreat, to the YoMoms and the Blessed Wives (esp. Lenka Golovlev); and to the fam: my mom Patti Chiarelli, my big bro Joe Perry, and my sweetest-most-fantastic-crazy-amazing etc. kids—Luc and Chloe.

Finally, thank you thank you thank you Pat Detlefsen for your *shimjung*! Love forever to my beloved, my true: Sebastien; and,

*kamsahamnida Omonim!*

Table of Contents

PART ONE

| | |
|---|---|
| The Fool | 11 |
| Getting to Know You | 12 |
| Wreck Things | 13 |
| Choice Words | 15 |
| The Clinch | 16 |
| Why *mate for life?* Red crown crane | 17 |

PART TWO

| | |
|---|---|
| Fool's Errand | 21 |
| In the War | 23 |
| Hansel & Gretel | 28 |
| Sound | 30 |
| Garden Apartments in Canoga Park, California | 32 |
| Passing Time | 34 |
| Grace | 38 |

PART THREE

| | |
|---|---|
| Vespers | 43 |
| Little's Lane in Peabody, Massachusetts | 46 |
| There was this egg. | 48 |

## PART FOUR

| | |
|---|---|
| Five Card Tarot Spread | 53 |
| Rooting | 56 |
| Zero Point | 57 |
| Trust | 59 |

## PART FIVE

| | |
|---|---|
| Brief History of Breath | 63 |
| Last but First | 64 |
| The Women | 66 |

## PART SIX

| | |
|---|---|
| The Prisoner | 71 |
| Her Children | 72 |
| Crave | 74 |
| Some thoughts on rocks: | 75 |
| Structural Integrity | 77 |

"Zero's the hero"

~kids

# PART ONE

# THE FOOL

Every fool knows death is change. So,
after the quake struck I dreamt "the Tower" card—
man and woman leaping off
Los Angeles skyscrapers; knock down
dragouts then over, and over. "Death." Though,
no sound resolution on the ground
that I could see as I rose in an elevator
as parsed, essential selves—
as *Will* in horse stance, who wore my face
and gripped her bullwhip; as *Intellect*,
this erect Hitchcock blond, clean and
suited up; as *Emotion*, a squat
sniveling tempest, a slave. There was something
for all of us on the top floor
where the door pinged open to a
harrowing, a rending love—and me
on the phone with a future self, who said, *Sorry,
but you're gonna die.* OK,
I shrugged, and woke
then broke-up with my then
life. Took off. Like "the Charioteer,"
a solo soldier, I began
converting engrams, forgiving parents,
landing–a degree, a career—a perceptible
*thud*. But this was before we married
my love, when I was still so old
I could not stand at the altar
and–like a Tarot "Fool"—amble off an edge into

# GETTING TO KNOW YOU

Remember yesterday, when an 8.8 hit Chile
and the earth's axis tilted?

800 died and
the days became shorter

by 1.26 milliseconds.

Remember before I met you? There was a time
they told me about you.

How the teenage you tossed grapes to hovering gulls
when out at sea. How you hooked one grape
and tugged a floating gull behind the tacking boat
called New Hope.

They told me you ate raw bacon.

How your mom made you

wear your hair in a bowl cut.
Now you're blushing.

Thank you.
The days are longer

now.

# WRECK THINGS

The last time we were driving in the city we fought over words
I can't remember, nearly careening off an onramp.
He insisted I said yak yak and meant blah blah, vice versa, and so
rim and axle were wrecked. Our car shambled
down to a city mechanic and crashed
at his place for the weekend. I was stunned silent, imagining
our Blazer in flight. Apparently—triumphantly—
some lowdown spirits attached to city-stink and domestic ferocity
had slyly spurred us, hoping against hope
to reaffirm their own earthbound happenstance,
their own sad resignations.

But this week—this time
on our toes—we crossed the bridge, skipping over the city.
And I warned those pitiful spirits, *We're here to play
together.* We all behaved. We let the radio talk
and drove straight to Ocean Beach where half way down Pier 42,
a few notes I had taken—incomprehensible
villanelle conception or grocery list—came loose,
lifted off. So, I stepped out on the water

at once. We had come to an open space
long the quay, where fishermen could cast long lines out to the
      farthest
possible facade of the sea;
where the splintered barrier wood dwindled, unable to keep me in
a standstill. My first step on water was for balance—
my arm arced, clutching after the folds of those notes.
The second step, for fright, caught me fast—
divided between two surfaces. This seemed wrong so I tiptoed,
following the paper's flux for a few yards,

scooping it up when the wind was lazy.

It didn't take long to come back. I hauled myself onto the pier.
He'd been watching. Maybe other people were watching.
He said, *I don't believe you*
*almost let it get away.* I shook my head and opened my mouth,
then closed it. Not one spirit clamored through salt-air to speak,
not one battered grandmother, jilted great-aunt, ancient suicide
      maiden
came around to spit through me, join me, wreck things.

# CHOICE WORDS

I love that word—
*expletive*. Terrible
substitute for the color others
love, but what a wonderful shape
between bared teeth! Lips getting screwed
tight to the gumline...You threw
so many my way
in Kyoto. We were pretty crabby back then—
a too new twosome
weighted under a sultry noon, flight lagged,
caffeine free, meatless, in a nicotine fit...
Well, you were really, so I was
getting a gust of hell—
a man-size tantrum. You said (stuff) and, *I'm leaving
RIGHT NOW!* As if
you could walk over an ocean
like the Pacific. I rushed
over your *pht pht* spewing;
said, *I love you. I love you. I love you...*

to the cumulous pagodas hovering above
you in the vast cobalt
Kyoto heaven. To that cool...
And these words, really
the first and best between us so far,

shut your mouth.

# THE CLINCH

In my turn I look for love in Nature,
though—all those cycles, mewing hues
and roaring scents, the grain of everything—

it does not seem to suffer love. The thing is,

I know Nature can mean
the man found last night
when I lifted the down cover and stole
near the heat he'd made.

His arms pitched out,
swaddling my torso,
one forearm across my spine,
behind my heart, wrenching me
to him and his cedar hazel smell,
to his plush lips mumbling,
*You were not here—I could not sleep.*

Letting my weight marry into that
clinch, I knew Nature
suffered me.

# WHY *MATE FOR LIFE?*  RED CROWN CRANE

prefer to
winter on that cold frontline.
In the rice stalks and creep sedge
that is the Cheorwon Basin—
between severed lovers
North and South
Korea. They
arc stemmed necks,
duet and prance, then nest
in the DMZ, bearing two eggs—
one of which survives. One egg

death, one life. Together,
the cranes mean "fidelity,"
risk. A lover may depart,
stunned and cut by a copter—
from North or South—
a frosted wing
broke, blood spent,
the living crane keening. Wild
grief for life—
she is broken
too. We'd rather break ourselves,

we'd rather be true South,
our backs to true
North, as if there never was
one hale body, one language:
*Why risk living*
*so near peril? What if*
*he won't love me later?*

*What if his Grim
rises out of the bog, strikes
early?* It strikes me
the cranes together mean,
also, "eternity." Hereafter—

the ever answered unison caw,
the tireless coupling,
the neck-twining
into one
ebon peninsula
as intimate affirmation
of peace.

# PART TWO

# FOOL'S ERRAND

I don't want to go home.

But I'm a Fool—my kind journeys. And,
like the Hierophant says, *What we resist persists*. So,
it's no wonder I dreamt the trek. It began
with Tituba, the original witch,
snuggled up on our all-weather porch seat
on our red, wood slat balcony in Salem.
She had my hawkish profile
against the royal hue of an autumn night—a strong moon
shine reflecting off my forehead.
And because she'd atoned
all our flagrant storytelling
sparking death, a rather cozy gnostic
voice moved through her, through us,
and the divide. *Go there
and get it*, we said, *Go
get it!* So,
I flew and set down in the western shadow valley
cradling my hometown,
set one foot in front of the other
in that uber "fool's errand," in pursuit of:
*it*. I soon found
freight train tracks cutting through golden tumbleweed
hills about to spark.
High in the hike, a rocky dead end pass
suddenly blackened and a lofty tunnel opened up
around the track. Stepping into that ink,
I moved away and away
from the dim day—
till a sudden turn in the corridor veered

and I could not see either end of the passage.
I did not know what I would stumble on.
Cougar, sumac, specter, vagrant?
The walls were flat without crevice or nook
to scurry into when a train came.
The air swelled with creosote, urine, musk. The creeping,
scraping ground, the beating overhead, the breath of
creatures—all of it dried my tongue, iced my sweat—
I could only hold my own arms. And that turn,
curving on and on like a curse,
finally tired me out. I had to sit
on the worn rail with my fright
to wait and see.
Aren't we supposed to see after time spent in the dark?
An air blew then
out the deep night below my throat, through the trumpet
portal of my mouth—it sounded
like finely honed scat, like a dog, like a small
comfort. What was I carrying around inside?
What companion sang and strolled in a tunnel in the mountain
of myself? If only I could believe that
I wasn't alone here, believe that
around the dark was a light
I'd come from, that could be returned to
and reveled in—if only I could allow any present underlife
to be one more place I moved through,
simply a means.
Then I could get up and go
*get it.*

# IN THE WAR

I.

When I was twelve I willed the soldiers home.

All the men were bright and rank,
and frayed—and blood
flowed from their hearts unbound.

They'd died of shrapnel or honor,
toxin or friendly
fire. These spirits named and numbered
deaths by your side, dad, deaths
by your hand,
during the eon of your two tours.

Still, I could not understand the conflict—
*Viet Nam.*

I needed endless intel, and your men
to be my men and in their camo
loom above me at the school library,
echo the barbed text in murmurs,
lead me through warfare and weather, through white
lies in letters home. They helped me
find the hills and huts

you conquered
by chance, in wonderment, by force.

II.

It was easy, dad,
to believe in you because you lived

a wizened parallel half-life
across town—in Hollywood, forever
in-country—
drinking your days away
for my sake, maybe

desperate to fill my absence.

In those days I'd curl
on a chair in my living room, cool and away
from the scorch
of a San Fernando Valley summer cig alert.

Fully giddy, my spirit would crouch
and conspire with those red
and flesh and black
and blue fellow combatants.

We soldiers
then launched standard mission procedure: *Prisoner of war!*
they whispered, *You are one of us.*
Or, *You must
suit up. When he departs, you will be the only one
who can save him.*
This was what I had always wanted!

To know your jungle just enough to pull you
out with pincers, to pull you out
whole and mewling

and at my unformed mercy.

III.

When I turned eighteen, they said, *It's time*

*for search and rescue.* So, I gathered my self
away from my solid, still form on the chair—
my spirit stood with them,
as tall and square boned.

Then, a grunt named Joe, just like you
dad, took my lucent hand and bade me leap
through the carpet, then the concrete,
till we struck soil and traveled southwest
bypassing pearlescent grubs essential for decomposition.

Soon, we launched out of earth,
through the hardwood lobby floor of the Hastings Hotel—
one of Hollywood's un-retrofitted relics
housing hookers, actors, and castaways
in its dull efficiencies.

I arrived unarmed,
hoping the troll recon said was you was not
you. This troll seemed busy,
bloated, and badly hunched. Like me,

he had audible words for invincible invisible companions.

His hair was pomaded black,
long, magnetic. I let go of Joe,
set my sights on that scurrying thing and spoke

with what turned out to be your smooth voice

in my stiff mouth. Oh, you were lovely
if I looked away and only listened:

*You are not mine*,
the troll that was you whispered distinctly.

Swiftly, my own
invincible invisible companions scattered
like one body
hit hard by a betty bomb.

IV.

The Hastings Hotel door seemed to swallow
you—you left me
to find my way out of a lobby existence
again. On tenterhooks,

I ordered my grunts to stay
the course, and they clambered to me,
out from behind potted plastic plants
and from under scuffed ottomans. They wrenched me
down through the floor and the fault lines,

then up into a disfigured barroom
serving you the thick liquids of our Azor ancestry.

Our entire lineage drank through you—

I could see in you our kin layered atop one another,
numbing their own petty crimes,
their *saudade*.

*What he does for the Azor kin corrupts*

*their trust in him—their hometown hero,*
the soldiers reported, as I eyed the hoards
of thick haired pearl hunters and stocky fishwives
attached to you,
their infant eyes gaping.

Their eyes flashing
like drumfire through the pattern on my living-room carpet

back in the Valley where I woke
from the barroom visitation to spy my
beloved platoon.
I asked them if I was doomed
to be a crowded bar. They said, *When your father dies*
*the ancestors must possess you.*

*Understand, little soldier—*
*they will not be able to help themselves.*

I understood
that eventually you would acknowledge me—
you would live among their ranks
and I would order Abstinence and Attention
and possibly the dressing of all wounds.

# HANSEL & GRETEL

Their father fought in Viet Nam. He got sick. They met him once,
long ago. He seemed fine. They spent life with their mother.
      The girl read a lot
of toothpaste labels; Clorox, Woolite, Ipecac, and Tampax
instructions. *My father likes to read, so I am
a great reader.* She enjoyed this logic every morning
she locked herself in the bathroom. Her brother made a dummy of
      himself
out of clothes tucked under bedsheets so he could snake
visits with some too-young-tenement-twins. *My father is
a great joker, so I'm as funny as hell,* he thought in a back-alley,
avoiding security and a rival tenement gang. They expected to bump
into their father, to see
him sick. After all, he lived in Hollywood. And, they lived sort of
      close
in Canoga Park. *Couldn't he do us a favor
and walk around the corner?* they'd say. They'd see
their mom's old boyfriends taxiing down the sidewalk, full throttle
from her old halfway house; drunk like their father, but not sick
in his war sick way. *He'll see us
and scream, thinking we're the bloody children
of Mei Lei,* the brother joked.
*He'll choose to pretend
he doesn't know us, then, at the last minute, turn
around with a knowing look,* said the sister trying
to be as philosophical as her father was in one legend. They sat
      alone
after school on a corner. *You'll be a bum like him,* they told each
      other.
*He's not a bum, he's sick,* they retorted,
waiting for their mother to return, to turn the corner

in recognition, and bark orders before collapsing after a harsh split
shift. They navigated neighborhood side streets, shuffling,
lifting their chins to other teens, giving change
to the bums, giving all they could
hold out. The brother slipped off to shoot up with a tenement twin
and the sister read Harlequins under covers, avoiding
the lazy gaze of her mother's newest monster
truck loving boyfriend. He'd come in and out
of her room like the others—always violently
philosophical. *Put that book down and let me
tell you what's what.* But, she was full up
bursting with her father's war. Still, those boyfriends insisted
she could take new forms (mother or lover or soldier?).
She told her brother. He laughed, *You're such a joker.*

# SOUND

In those years I did not sleep.
If I slept I missed him more—missed the night
copters whirring near city ground, near
our terrible home, my fatherless home.
Missed those hopped up news-copters,
those quick cop-copters mega-phoning
and floodlighting our lots and potholed pathways,
the bedroom windows and eyes
of capped rough boys running. I know enough

to know my soldier father
lay under this same fast hack at air—years before
I was born—under a *whickachop whickachop whickachop*.
He lay lucid in those humid 'Nam
war nights—swallowing
hard against acid,
sweat pooling in the pits,
sliding down the slight spine. My long lost father
with this same upchucked gut.

And stuck—apart, in our own time—we'd wonder,
*Who, by morning, would be left?*
*And what does it matter?* We'd both rise—deadish—
and he'd wander away the rest of his days
like Cain—in and out of Veteran's hospitals.
I'd spend my days waking waking shaking
off his old sound waves, mine. We were one
on a single frontline—all the people
along that front, at war
across time. I am more

awake now, living
with my children, my husband—moved
away from a constant copter chop. Now, ocean sounds—
fake ones at least—ease me into sound sleep.
They wash me
into an ancient whole night
or moment—when, as a baby, I lay in an open dresser drawer
in a flat half-a-block from Venice Beach. Where—
after warring, after sun
tacos beer mother
*mother mother—*

he sighed in a soft bed.

# GARDEN APARTMENTS IN CANOGA PARK, CALIF.

*1. Friends*

    We didn't go too far
back into the tenement. We knew a curious woman
had been shot by stray bullets; poking
her entire torso out a window, she invited in

too much information. We didn't dare speak
full words, or open our faces
in recognition. We squinted if we were smart.
We pretended to believe all bravado—all bruises
heroic, all bones twisted
in triumph against brass knuckles

and the whole of a nameless
gang. If we were weak we made friends
elsewhere, culling from the houses
or duplex condos with foyers, chandeliers, blinds
and two incomes. But that was rare.

*2. Family*

    Our mothers spent stamps.

    Our mothers sagged in posterns,
bummed smokes, talked crap, cocked chins
to each other— to liars
and lairless losers, ex-husbands and each baby's daddy.

    We saw our mothers as the evenings turned—
lips serrated,

eyes lit by sitcoms.

We'd watch their halos bloom
as stains of nicotine fanned out
on walls above wicker chairs facing kitchen windows—
each crown illuminating
jowl rage.

Everyone forgot how young they were,
how close.

3. *Home*

     Some of us and our squalling
children eventually moved upstairs or out back
into the dead woman's place—
her threadbare yellows and thick reds
long since coated over.

     We'd live with local boys,
having had sex as soon as we could
be ashamed of being left
out—as soon as we were twelve, at least.

     We tried to wait
in laundry rooms, cracked courts, blind alleys.
We waited for someone
to get a car, to get out.
Still, our souls—like our mothers—
called the Garden home.

# PASSING TIME

On a loop at the end of a rope
that hung from a jut of rebar
at the top of a train tunnel façade,

we'd fit and fashion a cardboard square
like the seat of a swing. Tasha and I
straddled that passage like pumas on crags
while my brother Joe pulled at Rick
—seated fast in the loop—
back along a plateau on the right side rock face
flanking the penny strewn tracks.
We watched Joe let go
and Rick whoop across the gape
then kick off the left side face and swing back
scrambling. Without Joe to catch him, Rick would lose
height, swing light, then hang
still, at the tunnel mouth, waiting for the train
to strike. There never was time
to shimmy out and leap over tracks,
and break bones in the leaping.

    \*


They began to time their trick to the oncoming
trains—when engines entered the rear of the tunnel
the boys swung and shouted the fat number
they got off. Five swings was the record
in the beginning.

    \*

Soon they tied a second noose
and swung in from either side of the hole.
Tasha and I held them and learned
to let go. We got strong.
We named the things
chariots, as in, *The second chariot must swing lower
to avoid each other, duh.* We'd get off
at least four synced swings,
the boys high-fiving as they crossed in the middle
before the roaring of the killer
winded past, hot and full of life.

   *

Soon six swings was the record. And I craved
a shot but the guys said no.

Somehow they could say no. No
Matter—Tasha and I could see each other

broken against a snub nosed Amtrak,
our brown hair and blood bouncing off thick windows
guarding gaping people
heading away.

So we kept swinging boys
till seven was the record.

   *

We all called it

*passing time.* Alone,
the boys called it *hypnotizing trains.* And Tasha
called it our *killing
spree.* "Your mom's gonna kill me,"
I'd tell Rick as he was on his way out
for the last time
that day. But she wouldn't. Not for this.

I remember his sister and his mother—
white trash knocked about by the men
they loved—how Rick came begging
at our window at dinner time.

How we'd feed him our spaghetti.
How he wanted to know his father's name…

*Lucky
bastard…*

    *

"You're gonna die,"
I started whispering to Rick
when eight was our best.
And it felt good in my body to mean this.
There was bliss in sweating and squatting and yanking
those boys back over the red boulders and scruff.

I didn't need to be at the end of a rope
to get high.

*

My belly has since gone soft around that old roiling delight
that made my core so hard.

Not soft so much as numb,

like a father  in a lean-to under an overpass,
or face down
near the tap at Gold Diggers. Like a father
in my bed.

*

When he went for a ninth
Rick begged me to swing him. He was barely a boy then.
He'd be a father soon. "Don't worry," he said
but I wasn't worried.  I was ready—I was weak
and I let go.

It was a win-win.

# GRACE

*1. Indian Summer*

     We heard rumors of razors in apples
and needle holes in wrappers.

Yet, we peeled a trillion sweetmeats
hungrily, as a three alarm fire
gnawed at the San Fernando Valley hills

on Halloween. The smoke

tumbled right
into nearby Simi Valley where rich folks lived
in stucco split levels
just below the old Manson Family caves.

We knew, where there's smoke
there's snakes—
rattlers, copperheads and more settling over Simi

like the black billows.
You just can't tell where

the wind blows, I guess.

*2. Trick or Treat*

     That year, we were homespun
pirates or gypsies
draped in fool's gold.

We were cheap sheet-ghosts—
our pillowcases nearly empty for taking
in the skyline. Flames

fanned the air in praise.
They hustled—made a halo of those sharp licks—
while buckling brush clapped

and free candy paled
when free candy was everything to us.

We lay in bed before they snuffed the fire—

*3. Lights Out*

we lay open
armed in the relative dark,
our bellies gnashing and moaning
for food, our weak teeth chewing one last
Tootsie pop or Skittle.

We needed more
jaw breaking treats to last like this
mean season

gone gracious.

We needed every red-engine knell to slumber
and a neighborhood cease-fire

and then we could wake stoked
to survive—stretch and run

into the All Saints Day dawn.

# PART THREE

# VESPERS

1.

You scheme, You
incite some dogs—

my phantom kin—who spur
a flash

rabbit to gallop
through hardened, high tide

zephyrs. I know I know
this animal.

She flies like a Fool—in a way
she never would were it not for fear.

2.

I think,
*I might move.*

I mean East,
towards his old cold hometown
Providence, where

I might
never unearth
the whole man
before the war. But, as the Father

of my father and his fathers, You unfurl
answers through circumstances:

> I watch one dun rabbit
> torn apart by dogs
> snuffling Pacific brush.

3.

I confess, I love

this dirty city, this West,
and don't want to move

East—because, when leaning
against the end, against the sway
of a westward pier, I know

my wounds are reliable. Still,

if I stay here I stay
exactly the same:  moved

by the ghosts of emotions so old
they seem as native
as California palms.

4.

You've sent an almost anti-gull, a colossal
sea eagle

to sound the alarm.

We're to end our vespers, begin our vigil—
like crossing a line in the sand.

I stand
and we three watch a great flame set
beneath the water line.

In the dark
we set off.

# LITTLE'S LANE IN PEABODY, MASS.

      Moms with men
with single moms—I've known these
slight girls trudging
the length of Little's Lane
to that tilted beige building
with its first story glass gash.
      All year round, on foot,
they pass the iron basement grate—that dank vast cage
restraining
contrabanded sunshine
canaries—the men's domain. These girls
lope like my mother.
They unwind
from second or third shifts,
their infants lulled by bent dark
grandmas. Their infants cling like I clung
to aged aromas—powder and spice—
through colic and longing.
      Their muggy men lounge
in the lot with cars on blocks,
on all long days. I hate them
letting beautiful toddlers run at my car
when I creep past, staring, my crimson car
rocking over ruts
and deep depressions on Little's Lane.
      *Someone take a stab!*
*Move!* I want to say, *Patch that window wound,*
*that eye-sore, with duct tape*
*on radiating fissures.*
      But I know Peabody,
and all these parts of towns

—even now
winter busts in
past glass incisors and curtain tongues.
      Peabody breeds
paralysis. And later, the concrete breath of summer—
that boil, that hornet—
will gust hard into the unmindful maw,
choking and keeping
every last innocent
ignorant.

## THERE WAS THIS EGG.

Thin skinned, heavy set, brown, not enough
for a meal. Like me it lingered
a foot to the left of the muddle—whole
somehow, abiding
when others, strewn about the wreckage, suffered cracked
ribs, spines, noses. My mother—
turvy, and hemmed upside down by the safety belt—
my mother in forced surrender—amped up
her usual banshee babbling. I remember
my annoyance kicking in.
I remember too her long labor
to save, to have us

here—just past Needles, just shy of Yucca
and that grand auburn canyon brimming with lichens,
yarrow and fishhook cacti. We never saw those cacti.
I saw my big brother dumped
atop the dislodged back windshield.
Around his palsic form, dollops of scarlet
condiments had sprung without ceremony
from the maw of our flung cooler.
His vertebrae rattled, his right arm bone showed.
A spilt wine sunrise stained the ample blue above us—
and that lone egg cast a shade.

Had it been third in the back row of the carton?
Was that it?
And, when chucked from slumber
by the flipped truck, did it roll out onto a loaf of bread,
roll along the length of our plush torn tent,
then over amber ground? What grace knew

it would not wobble? And, with the rising desert blaze,
did it soon hard boil? My own form, cast

a long shade too. Was it a permanent stain, rippling
across the rocks? Is that how I am, where I am?

I want to be where
my nerve's up, be west again,
driving up alongside that bone-whole, stunned girl.
Say, *It's me—I mean us. Hop in.* And she'd come,
with the shade of the egg in her hand.
She'd sidle away from the wailing vista
of our brother, pale and prone—
and we'd talk about eighth grade, about how hard it is
to stop playing "let's pretend."

We'd zoom forward, and find ourselves
at that canyon of crimson monkey flowers,
at that rocky wide of skyrocket and toadflax.
We'd swipe at our sweat at the precipice—and together
fling that egg in air, watch it hatch
and fly. A phoenix? A dove?
The canyon's own peregrine falcon? It doesn't matter—
each time I think of the egg I insert a new bird.

# PART FOUR

PART FOUR

# FIVE CARD TAROT SPREAD

Oh, Fool. You've got the "Death"
card. You've got travel plans,
oh chopper pilot. To crash
and make death mean
change, you need to lose
your back rotor, swivel and nod
nose down
so the blades face a mountain of pines,
so the blades shield your cabin from
razored branches.

You need the departed
son of the old folks in seats 7A and 7B.
You need that son who had the heart
attack—to stand in a spoke-wheeled vehicle;
to grip a helm of ether
and wield a fierce
pair of sky mustangs;
to stretch out his foot through incoming fog
and kick that rotor off. This "Charioteer" will
reign in your Sikorsky 92.

Collide then
with a lone cherry tree
in tuning fork form—the trunk, sprouting
from thick mist, will keep you. It must
be firm, be gripped—
by a fist sprouting out a white billow,
by the "Ace of Wands" who
is one more son of those
ancients. This one dead from a roof top fall.

This one clutching at the copter's drop
four stories above clouded
ground. Your craft must slam
then. Slam into a muddy cradle.
It will not explode

yet. The exit hatch will ease
open. The bent catch lifted by a wind, by another
brother—ages ago crushed
by a truck on Route 9.
Your hand will be taken by him
in the dim toward that door
—as if this "Magician"
cast the force of mystery against

fear. Inside the hull,

attendants for the eldest, and nannies for the youngest,
will release their charges
at once, carry them out to gloom and drizzle.
Each of your battered sixteen will crawl
in muck,
down the slope—away from sudden, late flames.
The grizzle grey grandfather will crawl. This is your father.

This is not your father. This is your father. He
won't ever say he thought he'd die by
fire weather misshapen metal…
By then he'll have offered his life so many times—
this "Hierophant" jailed seven times and beaten for his family:
during home invasions, and when the rack and whip
of war torture reared. But,

he'll think this outcome
curious. *Don't you think this life curious?*

he'll whisper at a web of branches,
his face bruised and damp with the breath
of the forest.

# ROOTING
~*for Pat Detlefsen*

Root for the nipple, root for the home team,
root your foot
and ground
when crisis strikes. Root in your trash
for treasure. But, the root of all evil
is uprooting—and always thinking,
*I've got no trash,* or, *I come from me.*
Fool—this just means you're numb
to the root
that binds our family.

# ZERO POINT
~*for Luc*

We never talk about the zero—
it's always *one two three*
*smack!*
lesson learned—

he's two and will be three, once was one
but never naught, or motherless,
he believes, never breathless
in a dream before tumbling in
to my womb—

and, when I slam the door
committing our first strongest
separation, he doesn't understand
he is at zero
again, choosing: me,
how I care and control, and
—I confess—

resist him as I was resisted
by my own gods—those other
dynamos who waited
at zero, their patience run out—
like those parents of yours

who cramped up,
frozen runners at their mark,

anticipating knowledge
(from God knows where)
to grow themselves
up past the unavoidable
lineal fear of giving
and receiving love.

# TRUST

     Damn lightning. Strobing
behind thin curtains.

I try not to see. I fitful twist
on the mattress, face down. But the bright

thrusts!

     I gotta get up
to pretend to comfort the kids.

My way is lit lit lit. Damn
windows.
Letting in every *FRAK!*

*FRAK! FRAK!* Why do we love
having too many windows?

     Were we were made to expose ourselves
to breaking mornings
on a top floor target? *FRAK!*

     My girl's in my boy's room under her *blankie*.

She perks up when I bust in
trying to hide  my hyper-breath.
She giggle-hops
on the bed with my son who, face on glass,
strains to see. He spools facts
on summer-bolt this. And, ball-bolt that.
Struck-ratios and burns and *FRAK!*

*FRAK! FRAK!*

    I lay down
with my heart—a pinball against the rib cage, a dervish

without God. I am the only one

thundering.

# PART FIVE

# BRIEF HISTORY OF BREATH

In the beginning, Nor'easter Winds breathed into flaccid bodies till
each solar plexus thrust love up through crowns billows mist, into
the providence for the start of sound—
till we exhaled venom in a long fall away from the Other and east;
then, in Siberia, pining for the Father, heartbroken herders
remembered the Mother by folding their throats into two tones
for eons till flutes and yidaki arrived in mind, in hand, as the holy
bones and whittled trees
we broke from Her body; later, Saxon monks on Britannia penned
songs and psalms scops learnt by heart by breathing a brace of
waddling vowels, by breaking all ranks in half—
like the arm of a monster broke by the huffing grunt of a hero—
like the sob of a peace-bride taken by brothers; soon, Sinatra
stretched all chords as if trumpeted by Dorsey and famously
mobsters from every shade reveled in this air while a million moll
wannabes swooned—their brains deflated into first faints, into
minor forms of first love; and here I am,
a breathless Fool—a pregnant Fool
and my child's major first love form; my form: slung over
the earth, over that mother
like an inverted sousaphone, spread wide like that gentle wife
of Tuba—here I am, into my tenth month, upturning lies I teach
my child with every short-of-breath that lets fear of love lock
my ribs against His second-wind.

# LAST BUT FIRST

*The workers who were hired about the eleventh hour came and each received a denarius. So when those came who were hired first, they expected to receive more. But each one of them also received a denarius… So the last will be first, and the first last. ~ Matt 20: 9-16*


The secret last but first legend of men is wrought from the favorite
    of a crouching grudge from an elder
One who plows sweats offers & the younger wily un-athletic well-lit
    second son struck dead terrible

Terrible garroting in the field by the elder because their parents
    know too much about ripe things so
A spare heir plods on immutable mute surviving barely keeping
    suicide at bay with lineal urge (and worse

There is a secret secret last/first legend of women begat by a
    handmaid begat by the mama of monotheism

Their kitchen spite the root of a later siege of an elder sister given
    as a trick hating like a holy war spark
When her cute little sister balancer of clay water jars & sacred
    nations is desired earned taken favored

& maid & mama cut-throat keen through their boys making it a
    man legend in the end a scrambling
For birthright with younger/elder half-brothers bombing each
    other for a few millennia) so one day

One of them is you my dear mentor my words surpassing yours in
    truth & beauty & you turn terrible

Terrible jealous enough to nail me in your so-so seller so I turn low
    write mean like you without dignity

Our faces sagging with the hideous pull of hate in a prior garden
        where I (as woman as up-start writer or
Other) should being last but first not wait eternity to love the
        unloved weight of you your terrible wound

# THE WOMEN

Kicking up the dust,
full of a word
feast, the desert gotten behind,
He ambled along
a feral trail weaving
out of the West rough
country, onto the coast
line of the Sea
of Galilee, through its wash
and rumble rhythms.
There, He cast a cadence,
a hook, at the hungry.
And the women were hungry.
They did not sleep fast in the family
mud flat. Their men rolled over after love
while they lay awake in the night,
damp cloth in hand,
the *Gennesaret* freshwater soothing
raw fishwife thighs. After love
the women sat up,
peered over shrouded sills
at shadows taking shape at dawn.
Did He sit on a stool and wait? How long
did the sleepwalking, bone tired
men take
to leave each morning? What word
caught the women then,
drew them to Him?
Close as a stone's throw,
as an infant
slung crosswise in a bright

taut shawl,
they huddled to him as if flush
against a milk full areola.
Did they understand
who they could be? All I know
is–later, I arrive
home from work
with sodden cotton nursing pads
over hot cracked nipples,
and I understand I need my baby
to suckle
the weight away—her taking
is salvation.

# PART SIX

# PART SIX

# THE PRISONER

Why poetry? Because content needs form.
And form needs attention. An inmate
in Hungnam, in the waning days of the Korean War,
washed his red chapped, limeburned body
with half his water ration. He stretched
pectorals, hamstrings, and psoas
before dawn while the whole death
camp slept—the inspired air elongating
his ligaments and stamina. When form is attended
content rises from a deep. The mayflies can be seen
mating in flight, in the latrine. It is a kind of love
in the sulfate mist. It is enough—
hefted he can heft 130 bags of acidic manure
from conveyor belt to truck. From conveyor belt to truck
he took care with 40 kilo bags of crystalline
crap sent to feed the gardens of his enemies.
He took on the tonnage of his team,
converting their 8 hours unto death
into five unto life. These fast friends
sat out the day meters away from an ammonia surge,
their broken skin weeping blood
slower in the lightening, in the little coup,
in the cold. Anything can be shared with the other.
Even half his rice ration. *Less is more*
he said, blooming. Even prayers in prison
can be sung for the other; imagine,
he sang to his beloved Hananim,
Heavenly Parent, *Don't worry about me...* Imagine,
I pour forth content into this container
and the poem lives and gives,
meaning I'm set free. This too is a miracle.

# HER CHILDREN

*What is it that changes when a poet becomes a mother?*
*~from "The Other Sylvia Plath" by Eavan Boland*

That bell jar—we adored it!  Peering in, peering out–

every coed doe
dutifully forgetting the suicide,
the way she let us see her bent like that
(our own mother!)

as if she were merely a man eating
Skylla, as if she were one of those prolific women

writers without children
(Dickenson, Moore, Bishop, et al.)
who stormed up their careers
wielding time like a sword.

As if she were never really prolific,
teeming with offspring,
with artless labor pain
and its reverb through her pen,
through all our doltish pens.

*No!*

She was always our Athena,
who we say bore down
like Daddy—her own boy

or girl shunted through air from mind,
but mortified,

slick with plum placenta,
the eyes of these poems black like beetles.

*Oh!* essentially loveless Athena—in February,
in the delivery room, by candlelight,
divorced,
at war with perfection—you cannot help that

we never knew you.

We only adored like daughters do
when biting on a potent teat.

# CRAVE
~*for Saint Rita, Patroness of the Impossible*

        Albino bees, like nascent holy words,
pattered out
her throat—out the pink
infant Rita—
tamped across her knobby gums
and blunt incisor buds…

They were buzzing brides
of Christ swarming
onto plush flush flesh…

*Think of them!* Strange

signs of a future fearsome
devotion. A movable feast
living, still, in Cascia in Umbria—
lighting on pilgrims and blossoms
in gardens outside Rita's abbey.
A movable feast for honey buzzards…

        My words are boney buzzards,
mealy verbage
launched from the shallow
nest of my mouth.
My words want meat—
her stingerless drones and
satisfaction–to know: *I am
ripe, understood…*

*I arrive.*

# SOME THOUGHTS ON ROCKS:

Which came first, the rock or the poem?

Ruth Stone (real name) says the poem
is
floating above us
coalescing like the unborn,
like ball lightning,
and if we don't run from the field to the desk
it won't inhabit us, erupt
from our pen.
It will spin away, bolt, to another
more willing more ready more swift
poet, or as some would say—
parent.

Ruth Stone wasn't much for research.
Whereas, I
know
I wanted to write about rocks,
so I look up how to make and wake
a model volcano
because
the only thing interesting about rock is how to
destroy it—
and those in the know
say you've got to heat it like a Mother
Earth's mantle chamber
to soften rock into magma.
Which I can't do, really, hence
the model—hence, *the remove.*

You know,
my son would like even fake magma.
He wouldn't care if it's just
water soap coloring vinegar
in a drink bottle—then, baking soda in a tissue
dropped into that bottle. "We *killed* it!"
I see us crowing.
And because I imagine the completed feat,
I feel a kind of triumph,
an easy triumph. Is that Ruth Stone's floating poem?
Is it like looking with love at
a gripped, mute photo
of your grinning kid—versus looking in
his eyes for real?

If that's Ruthy's schtick, that's sad.
Can't we both be right? Like how I got a C-section—
because I think too much.
It took two days of Mount Vesuvian pain, a spinal tap, and a slice,
to get this—rather cute—baby out.
While (true story here)
my more fluid friends
pulled into the nearest hospital parking lot,
where she *hhheeeee-*
*hhheeeeed* and *hwooooo-*
*hwooooooood*
through some "pressure" for ten minutes in the backseat
as he drove with his knees—
his left hand on the cell to the nurse,
his right hand reaching back
in time to catch
the baby.

# STRUCTURAL INTEGRITY

A universe walks into a bar, sits
down and says to the barkeep, *Just gimme*

*the usual.* Or, a Soul walks in
to a bar, says to herself, *How come you are*

*over there and I'm over here?* God walks
into this Universe, sits down and says

to all the people, *You wanna take this
outside?* Or God says, *Lend me an ear?* So,

an ear walks into a starry starry
night, sits down and says to the Artist, *You...*

*lose something?* Or a mouth gets near an ear,
sits down and says, *You hoo! Any body*

*home?* A home walks into a man, sits down
and sings, *Love me tender...* Or this Home walks

into a man, says to the feet, *Don't walk
away from me!* A marriage walks into

a bed, sits down and says to the couple,
*The inside is bigger than the outside.*

Or, *Love your enemy.* The enemy
makes his bed, lies down, and sighs, *I give up...*

About the Author:

Jennifer Jean's other poetry collections include: *The Archivist, Fishwife* and *In the War*; as well, she's released *Fishwife Tales*, a collaborative CD comprised of art songs and accompanied recitations. She is: a volunteer blogger for *Amirah*, a website advocating for sex-trafficking survivors; a principal organizer of the Massachusetts Poetry Festival; and Director of the Morning Garden Writers Retreat. Jennifer teaches writing and literature at Salem State University, and she lives in Salem, MA with her husband and two children.

For more about Jennifer Jean, visit: www.fishwifetales.com

## A Message from Jennifer Jean

Dear Reader,

I hope that reading this book has been a good experience for you. If it has, I expect that you can think of other people who would appreciate it. Here's how you could help them and me. Many books are competing for readers' attention, and the most important way for a book to get more notice is for readers to write favorable reviews and post them on Amazon.com.

The more positive reviews or comments a book gets, the more it moves up the ranking for exposure when people search on Amazon. When a book has ten reviews it becomes eligible to be included in the "also bought" and "you might like" recommendations. These listings add to the number of books likely to be purchased and read.

If you don't want to write a review, please take a few minutes to read and rate reviews posted by other readers. Just the act of "liking" a review moves books up the queue in which they appear.

Thanks in advance for your effort to boost the distribution and exposure of this book! I really appreciate it!

www.ingramcontent.com/pod-product-compliance
Lightning Source LLC
LaVergne TN
LVHW091318080426
835510LV00007B/535